THE LITTLE BOOK OF
CORBYN

Published by Orange Hippo!
20 Mortimer Street
London W1T 3JW

ISBN 978-1-91161-030-4

Editorial: Stella Caldwell, Victoria Godden
Project Manager: Russell Porter
Design: Tony Seddon
Production: Jessica Arvidsson

A CIP catalogue for this book is available from the British Library

Printed in Dubai

10 9 8 7 6 5 4 3 2 1

Jacket cover photograph: Theodore Liasi/Alamy Stock Photo

THE LITTLE BOOK OF
CORBYN

IN HIS OWN WORDS

CONTENTS

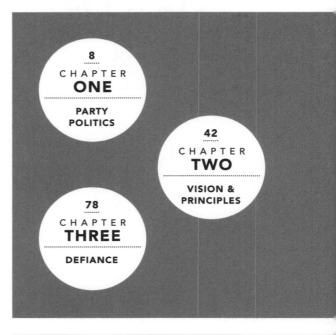

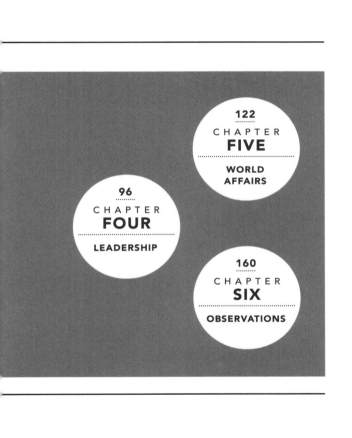

INTRODUCTION

For over three decades, Jeremy Corbyn was a little-known MP sitting on Labour's back benches. Seen as an old-fashioned socialist, he'd never held a position of authority in government and had voted against his own party an incredible 400 times. So, his rapid ascent to leader of the Labour Party in 2015 and then Prime-Minister-in-waiting was seen as nothing short of miraculous.

When Corbyn first entered the leadership race, bookmakers gave him odds of a hundred to one. But his anti-austerity, anti-war stance won him a huge following, especially among young people – and "Corbynmania" was born. In the 2017 general election, the shock result saw Labour's share of the vote increase by 9.6 per cent, the biggest swing since 1945.

A big part of Corbyn's appeal is his understated style and measured tone, his lack of arm-waving bluster. His critics have compared him to an ageing geography teacher – sincere but lacking in humour. It's true his speeches and media appearances aren't littered with witty one-liners or killer punch lines. But that's not what Corbyn's about: there is a steely conviction that runs through his words, an unbending belief that his politics hold the key to a better Britain. And he is a fighter: his survival of coup attempts, allegations that he supports Hamas or the IRA, and accusations of incompetence bear testament to that.

Corbyn's long career, addressing Parliament and protest rallies, and now at the helm of the Labour Party, has produced a wealth of fascinating and memorable quotes. And among them all, there is sometimes a glimpse of self-depreciating humour and of Corbyn the man.

CHAPTER
ONE

PARTY
POLITICS

66

The government may well
squeeze this nasty little measure
through the House tonight, but
the opposition that they have
created will live for a long time.
The unity of that opposition
will live for even longer.

99

Rate support grant debate,
House of Commons, 16 January 1985

66 Is the minister aware that he is getting a reputation for being a parsimonious philistine? **99**

Question to Mr Richard Luce MP, Minister for the Arts, during the public libraries debate, 8 February 1989

❝

It is the right of a democratically elected parliament to act in defence of our traditional liberties, and everything should be done to keep it that way. **❞**

The Guardian, *28 November 2008*

66

We need to be very careful.
Democracy is the issue, and
democracy ought to be the means
by which we decide these issues,
rather than secret negotiations
resulting in a fait accompli being
presented to us.

99

On services ownership,
House of Commons, 25 February 2014

❝

Marx analyzed what was happening in a quite brilliant way. The philosophy around Marx is absolutely fascinating.

❞

The Andrew Marr Show,
BBC One, 26 July 2015

66

It's been fascinating – and exhilarating – watching this movement mushroom over the last few weeks, this campaign is about spreading a message of hope and change based on the central choice – five years or more of continued austerity, or a plan for investment and growth that stands up for the majority.

99

Labour Party leadership campaign, 2015

66

We can win an awful lot of people into the political spectrum by offering something that is... radical.

99

Labour Party leadership campaign, 2015

66

Loyalty is about the party and the movement... if you want a better and more effective party, we've got to open ourselves up much more to our membership and our supporters. **99**

New Statesman, *29 July 2015*

66

I want to see a more collective style in how our party operates, in politics as a whole.

99

Evening Standard, *5 August 2015*

66 We are not doing celebrity, personality, abusive politics – we are doing ideas. This is about hope. **99**

The Guardian, *7 August 2015*

66

We're not going back anywhere,
we're going forward, we're going
forward in democracy, we're going
forward in participation, we're
going forward with ideas. **99**

The Independent, *9 August 2015*

66

We are all in the Labour Party because we want the Labour Party to be a vehicle for social change. There is a thirst for debate in the party, and all those who have joined haven't joined without a purpose.

99

Financial Times, *23 August 2015*

We challenge the narrative that only the individual matters, and the collective is irrelevant; instead we say the common good is the aspiration of all of us.

Labour Party leadership campaign, September 2015

66

Trade unions are a force for good – a force for a more equal society.

The Guardian, *13 September 2015*

99

66

So I thought my first Prime Minister's Question Time I'd do in a slightly different way and I'm sure the prime minister [David Cameron] is going to absolutely welcome this, as he welcomed this idea in 2005, but something seems to have happened to his memory during that period...

...So I sent out an email to thousands of people and asked them what questions they would like to put to the prime minister, and I received 40,000 replies. **"**

Debut as leader of the opposition at Prime Minister's Questions, 16 September 2015

66

I don't believe in personal abuse of any sort. Treat people with respect, treat people as you would wish to be treated yourself. Listen to their views, agree or disagree, but have that debate. There is going to be no rudeness from me...

…I say to all Labour activists, 'cut out the personal abuse, cut out the cyber-bullying and especially the misogynistic abuse online and let's get on bringing real values back into politics.'

99

Labour Party Conference,
29 September 2015

66

I think we should all be accountable to our parties, but I also think that accountability should be a process of engagement: that MPs do engage with their constituency parties, do engage with their constituents, and MPs do change their minds on things because of local opinion.

99

Huffington Post UK, *20 December 2015*

66

The Parliamentary Labour Party is
a crucial and very important part of
the Labour Party, but it is not the
entirety of the Labour Party. **99**

Newsbeat, *BBC One,*
29 December 2015

'United we stand, divided we fall' is one of the oldest and truest slogans of the Labour movement.

In response to the Brexit referendum result, June 2016

> "
>
> Labour has the responsibility to give a lead where the government will not. We need to bring people together, hold the government to account, oppose austerity and set out a path to exit that will protect jobs and incomes.
>
> "

In response to the vote of no confidence in Corbyn's leadership following the Brexit referendum, 28 June 2016

66

Labour Party members must all be free to criticize and oppose injustice and abuse wherever we find it.

99

Anti-Semitism speech, June 2016

66

There's no doubt my election as Labour leader a year ago and re-election this month grew out of a thirst for a new kind of politics, and a conviction that the old way of running the economy and the country isn't delivering for more and more people.

Labour Party Conference,
28 September 2016

99

"

Our country's history is based on individual ingenuity and collective endeavour. We are the country of Ada Lovelace, Alan Turing and Tim Berners-Lee, the land of Isambard Kingdom Brunel and Sarah Guppy, George Stephenson and Eric Laithwaite. The Tories have turned their back on this proud British tradition. They have put privatization and cutting spending first.

"

Labour Party Conference,
28 September 2016

66

I want everyone to put their views forward, every union branch, every party branch, so we develop organically the strengths we all have, the imagination we all have.

TUC Conference, 15 September 2017

99

66

It is often said that elections can only be won from the centre ground. And in a way that's not wrong – so long as it's clear that the political centre of gravity isn't fixed or unmovable, nor is it where the establishment pundits like to think it is. It shifts as people's expectations and experiences change and political space is opened up...

…Today's centre ground is certainly not where it was 20 or 30 years ago. A new consensus is emerging from the great economic crash and the years of austerity, when people started to find political voice for their hopes for something different and better.

99

Labour Party Conference, 27 September 2017

“

Our party must speak for the overwhelming majority in our country. Labour is a broad church and can be broader still. I lead in that spirit. After all, I appointed John McDonnell, despite him being a Liverpool fan, and even Andrew Gwynne, who supports Man City.

”

Labour Party Conference,
26 September 2018

"

[No-deal Brexit] won't return sovereignty, it will put us at the mercy of Trump and the big US corporations dying to get their teeth into our NHS, sound the death knell for our steel industry, and strip back our food standards and animal welfare protections.

"

The Independent, *26 August 2019*

66

The prime minister [Boris Johnson]
acted illegally when he tried
to shut down opposition to his
reckless and disastrous plan to
crash out of the European Union
without a deal. But he has failed.
He will never shut down our
democracy or silence the voices
of the people.

99

Labour Party Conference,
24 September 2019

66

My parents' generation fought
hard to establish the principle
of a universal health service
owned and run by the public.
They left it in our trust. It's our
duty to defend it. We will end
the sell-offs and privatization.
Our NHS is not for sale, not to
Trump or anyone else.

99

*Labour Party Conference,
24 September 2019*

CHAPTER
TWO

VISION & PRINCIPLES

> **"**
> Care for the elderly is an important issue. It cannot be left to volunteers, charities or to people going out with collecting boxes to see that old people are looked after properly. **"**

Care of the elderly debate,
House of Commons, 22 February 1984

66

It is sheer hypocrisy for Tory
members to blame the poor
unfortunate people who have to
sleep in cardboard boxes when
they themselves put those people
on the street, splash them every
night as they drive past in their
Porsches and kick dirt in the
faces of the poor.

99

Policing (London) debate,
House of Commons, 24 June 1988

66

Exactly what useful work did those stockbrokers do to gain their enormous wealth, other than to exploit the people who work in industry, to take their money away and to make no useful contribution to society?

99

Inequalities in London debate,
House of Commons, 12 July 1988

66

I shall not say that this is a
landlord's charter; it is worse
than that. It is a profiteering
landlord's charter.

Rent Officers debate,
House of Commons, 21 March 1989

66

Hunting with dogs and the vile killing for bloodlust in the name of sport should not be allowed in this country.

99

Abolition of Deer Hunting debate, House of Commons, 19 June 1990

It is important that politicians defend their ability to act without fear or favour, and it is in the public interest that they hold ministers and public servants to account.

Following the arrest of Damian Green over Home Office leaks, The Guardian, *28 November 2008*

66

When legal aid was first introduced in 1949, the late Arthur Skeffington said that the law at that time was like the Ritz, in that those who could afford to pay had access to it, while those who could not did not. Legal aid… is fundamental to giving everybody in this country access to justice.

99

Legal aid debate, House of Commons, 14 December 2010

66

Many people in my constituency come to see me absolutely distraught at the prospect of losing their private rented flat because of the imposition of a housing benefit cut. Social cleansing is going on in all of central London because of the benefit cap. That is a disgraceful situation.

99

House of Commons debate,
6 December 2012

"

What kind of city are we living in, if we encourage the development or ownership of large, expensive properties for investment and land banking... while people are sleeping on the streets?

"

London housing debate, House of Commons, 5 February 2014

We judge our economy not by the presence of billionaires but by the absence of poverty.

Labour Party leadership campaign,
22 July 2015

66

We are one of the richest countries in the world, and there is absolutely no reason why anyone should have to live in poverty. **99**

Labour Party leadership campaign, 2015

> **"**
> You grow your way to prosperity;
> you don't cut your way to it. **"**

Labour Party leadership campaign, 2015

66

I'll put this in black and white
now – it's absolutely disgusting,
the level of serious poverty in
Britain.

99

New Statesman, *29 July 2015*

"

It is unacceptable that many women and girls adapt their daily lives in order to avoid being harassed on the street, public transport, and in other public places from the park to the supermarket.

Policy statement, August 2015

> **"**
> I absolutely do not condone it
> [racism]… I have spent my life as
> a campaigner against racism; my
> parents were campaigners against
> racism. My mother was there in
> Cable Street alongside the Jewish
> and Irish people opposing the rise
> of Nazism in Britain. Anti-Semitism,
> Islamophobia, far-right racism
> is totally wrong and absolutely
> obnoxious.
> **"**
>
> The World at One, *August 2015*

66

There are some people who have had no pay rises for a very long time, and, working in highly skilled and highly responsible roles in the health services and education, they deserve to be properly remunerated.

99

The Guardian, *1 August 2015*

66

A more productive economy in the long term will bring us higher tax revenues, but that requires long-term investment in infrastructure and the skills necessary to grow a balanced economy.

99

London rally, 21 August 2015

66

I believe in public ownership, but I have never favoured the remote nationalized model that prevailed in the post-war era. Like a majority of the population and a majority of even Tory voters, I want the railways back in public ownership. But public control should mean just that, not simply state control: so we should have passengers, rail workers and government too, co-operatively running the railways to ensure they are run in our interests and not for private profit.

99

8 August 2015

❝

I say thank you in advance to us all working together to achieve great victories, not just electorally for Labour but emotionally for the whole of our society to show we don't have to be unequal, it doesn't have to be unfair, poverty isn't inevitable, things can and they will change.

❞

Labour leadership victory speech, 12 September 2015

I want us as a movement to be proud, strong and able to stand up and say we want to live in a society where we don't pass by on the other side to those people rejected by an unfair welfare system.

Labour leadership victory speech, 12 September 2015

“

Labour will oppose the Welfare Bill in full. We oppose the benefit cap. We oppose social cleansing.

”

TUC Conference, 15 September 2015

"

Young people and older people are fizzing with ideas. Let's give them the space for that fizz to explode into the joy we want of a better society.

"

Labour Party Conference,
29 September 2015

Since the dawn of history, in every human society there have been people who have been given a great deal and many more who have been given little or nothing... And time and time again, the people who receive a great deal tell the many, 'Be grateful to have anything at all.' They say the world cannot be changed and the many have to accept the terms of which they are allowed to live...

…Labour is the voice that says to the many at home and abroad, 'You don't have to take what you are given.' Labour says, 'You may be born poor but you don't have to stay poor.'

99

Labour Party Conference,
29 September 2015

I want to tackle one thing head on. The Tories talk about economic and family security being at risk from us and perhaps even more particularly from me. I say this to them: how dare these people talk about security for people and families in Britain? Where is the security for families shuttled around from one rented flat to another on six-month tenancies with children endlessly having to change schools...

…Where is the security for young people starting out on their careers knowing they are locked out of any prospect of owning their own home by soaring house prices? Where is the security for families driven away from their children, schools and communities by these welfare cuts?... That is the nub of it: Tory economic failure. An economy that works for the few not the many.

"

Labour Party Conference,
29 September 2015

66

You pay more in wages, get more in tax, you get people living a higher standard, you get more money. It's a kind of circle. **99**

Huffington Post UK, *21 December 2015*

> **66**
> Inequality is a terrible waste of time, a waste of people's resources. **99**

Huffington Post UK, *21 December 2015*

66

There's a lot of debate about what's happening in the Labour Party at the present time. ... But one [question] I got today really did puzzle me. They said, 'How are you coping with the pressure that's on you? I simply said this: 'There is no pressure on me. None whatsoever.' The real pressure... is when you don't have enough money to feed your kids, when you don't have a roof over your head, when you're wondering if you're going to be cared for...

...When you're wondering how
you can survive. You're wondering
how you're going to cope with the
debts you've incurred ...
That is the real pressure in
our society.

99

Durham Miners' Gala, 9 July 2016

""

Sorry, but we live in a democracy
and the government has to be
responsive to Parliament.

""

*On giving Prime Minister Theresa May
an ultimatum regards her intention to trigger
EU negotiations,* Sunday Mirror,
5 November 2016

66

We will fight with every last breath of our body to defend the principle of a healthcare system free at the point of need for everybody as a human right.

99

Speech to anti-Trump protesters, 4 June 2019

66

Today would have been the 90th birthday of Anne Frank had she survived… In her diary she wrote many things, but one of them that I think really does apply to all of us at all times is 'Human greatness does not lie in wealth or power, but in character and goodness.' I think we should remember her life and all that she's inspired in so many others ever since the Second World War.

99

Prime Minister's Questions,
12 June 2019

66

I am not prepared to stand by
while our NHS is sacrificed on the
altar of US big business or any
other country's big business.

99

Labour Party Conference,
24 September 2019

CHAPTER
THREE

DEFIANCE

Some colleagues have said
they would not be very keen on
working with me, but I am sure
these things were said in the heat
of the moment.

Labour Party leadership campaign, 2015

66

I was at the Battle of Britain memorial yesterday. I was there out of respect for that amazing moment in British history. I was also thinking about my family, my mum and dad who were there at that time in London, and worked as air raid wardens during the Blitz, and I was thinking about that. It was a respectful ceremony, and I stood in respect throughout it. **99**

On being criticized for not singing the national anthem at a memorial ceremony, 16 September 2015

66

I have already said and will continue to say that I won't respond to personal abuse, and I never make any personal abuse, ever, to anybody. I just don't do that kind of politics.

99

New Statesman, *23 September 2015*

> **"** I want to take this opportunity to apologize for not doing the decent thing and going back in time and having a chat with him about his appalling behaviour. **"**

After learning through the press that his great-great-grandfather, James Sargent, was the cruel manager of a Victorian workhouse, Labour Party Conference, 29 September 2015

66

You don't have to set limits on your talent and your ambition – or those of your children. You don't have to be grateful to survive in a world made by others.

99

Prime Minister's Questions,
4 November 2015

"

How dare these people talk about
security for families and people
in Britain? There's no security
for the 2.8 million households in
Britain forced into problem debt
by stagnating wages and the Tory
record of the longest fall in living
standards since records began.

"

On being labelled a security threat,
Prime Minister's Questions, 4 November 2015

> 66
>
> I was accused of not bowing properly to the queen. I decided I wouldn't respond. Had I responded, the debate would have been about at what angle one should bow.
>
> 99

Red Pepper, 21 December 2015

66

I decided to invite Donald Trump on his visit to Britain to come with me to my constituency because he has problems with Mexicans and he has problems with Muslims. As you know, my wife is Mexican and my constituency is very, very multi-cultural so what I was going to do was go down to the mosque with him and let him talk to people there.

99

The Andrew Marr Show, *17 January 2016*

"

I was democratically elected leader of our party for a new kind of politics by 60 per cent of Labour members and supporters, and I will not betray them by resigning. **"**

After losing a vote of no confidence,
28 June 2016

66

When it comes to Brexit, this
government has delivered more
delays and more cancellations
than Northern Rail.

99

Prime Minister's Questions,
6 June 2018

66

I regret that seven MPs decided
they would no longer remain part
of the Labour Party. I thank them
for their work. I hope they realize
they were elected to Parliament on
a manifesto that was based around
investment in the future; that
was based around a more equal
and fairer society; that was based
around social justice…

... – and it is that programme that we are going to put to the electorate in the future, that does have enormous support. They were elected to carry out those policies. They decided to go somewhere else.

99

19 February 2019

"
Theresa May should not be rolling out the red carpet for a state visit to honour a president who rips up vital international treaties, backs climate change denial, and uses racist and misogynist rhetoric. **"**

Twitter, 26 April 2019

Boris Johnson is part of an elite who think they can do whatever they like. He thinks he's above us all. He's not.

Twitter, 24 September 2019

66

Let me send this message to Boris Johnson: If you still lead your party into an election, we know your campaign will be swimming in cash. But we've got something you haven't...

...People in their hundreds of thousands rooted in all communities and all age groups across Britain, and we'll meet you head on with the biggest people-powered campaign this country has ever seen — and if we win, it will be the people who win.

Labour Party Conference,
24 September 2019

CHAPTER
FOUR

LEADERSHIP

I tend to see the best in people all the time. Is that a weakness? I don't know.

On being asked what his greatest weakness is, The Guardian, *17 June 2015*

"

I'm a leader, not a dictator. I want to persuade people rather than threaten or control them.

"

Democracy Now!, *August 2015*

❝

I am just an ordinary person trying to do an ordinary job.

❞

The Guardian, *7 August 2015*

If the leadership can't win a debate, then we should show true leadership and implement the democratic will of our party.

The Guardian, *26 August 2015*

> **"**
> After only two or three weeks in office, we discovered we had a backlog of 100,000 emails sent to me. We had a backlog of 1,000 invitations to speak at places all over the country – and all over the world, for that matter.
> **"**

Red Pepper, September 2015

“

For the absolute avoidance of doubt, my leadership will be about unity, drawing on all the talents – with women representing half of the shadow cabinet – and working together at every level of the party.

”

The Guardian, *13 September 2015*

66

I haven't had vast amounts of ministerial experience – in fact, none at all. But I do have a lot of experience of people.

99

The Observer, *26 September 2015*

66

The prime minister [David Cameron] is doing his best, and I admire that.

99

After hearing a lengthy response to a question about welfare reforms, Prime Minister's Questions, 14 October 2015

66

Could I bring the prime minister [David Cameron] back to reality?

99

On hearing the claim that house building under the Conservatives had reached record levels, Prime Minister's Questions, 14 October 2015

❝

I notice in some of the newspapers that they have taken a bit of an interest in me. According to one headline, 'Jeremy Corbyn welcomed the prospect of an asteroid "wiping out" humanity'. Asteroids are pretty controversial and it is not the kind of thing I would want to rule out... without a full debate at conference and a review, so can we have the debate later in the week?

❞

Prime Minister's Questions,
4 November 2015

I've been proud to be the chair of the Stop the War coalition, proud to be associated with the Stop the War coalition.

Stop the War fundraising dinner,
11 December 2015

66 The other side of it [leadership] is that decisions come to you and you have to take them. And I make mistakes like anybody else, I will make mistakes. And you have to reflect on it and you have to listen to people. That is the key. **99**

Huffington Post UK, *19 December 2015*

66

I'm carrying on. I'm making the case for unity, I'm making the case of what Labour can offer to Britain, of decent housing for people, of good secure jobs for people, of trade with Europe and of course with other parts of the world. Because if we don't get the trade issue right, we've got a real problem in this country.

99

Response to calls for his resignation following the Brexit referendum, Channel 4 News, 24 June 2016

66

If you do what you believe in,
you're strong. It's when you don't
do what you believe in that you're
weak. And we are strong.

99

The Independent, *16 May 2017*

> **"**
> I'm not a dictator who writes things to tell people what to do. **"**

Theresa May vs Jeremy Corbyn debate, Sky News and Channel 4, 30 May 2017

"

You should never be so high
and mighty you can't listen
to somebody else and learn
something from them. Leadership
is as much about using the ear as
using the mouth.

"

Theresa May vs Jeremy Corbyn debate,
Sky News and Channel 4, 30 May 2017

> **❝**
> The door of her [Theresa May's] office might be open but the minds inside it are closed and the prime minister is clearly not listening. **❞**

Exchange over May's request for Brexit cross-party talks, Prime Minister's Questions, 23 January 2019

66

I usually thank the prime minister [Theresa May] for an advance copy of her statement, but it was handed to me just as I was leaving my office to come down here. So I can only assume she entrusted it to the Transport Secretary to deliver it to me.

99

Referring to Transport Secretary Chris Grayling, House of Commons, 12 February 2019

66

Theresa May is right to resign. She's now accepted what the country's known for months: she can't govern, and nor can her divided and disintegrating party.

99

Twitter, 24 May 2019

> **The next PM should be chosen not by the US president, nor by 100,000 unrepresentative Tory Party members, but by the British people in a general election.**

Twitter, 1 June 2019

66

This is a government with no mandate, no morals and, as of today, no majority.

99

Following Tory MP Phillip Lee's defection to the Liberal Democrats, House of Commons, 3 September 2019

I am leading the party, I am proud to lead the party, I am proud of the democracy of the party and of course I will go along with whatever decision the party comes to.

Referring to the Labour Party's stance on Brexit, Labour Party Conference, 24 September 2019

66

This is an extraordinary and precarious moment in our country's history. Boris Johnson has lied to the country. The government will be held to account for what it has done. This unelected prime minister should now resign.

99

Labour Party Conference,
24 September 2019

66

I have what might be considered a different view of leadership from the one people are used to. I do believe leaders should have strong principles that people can trust. But leaders must also listen and trust others to play their part. Because there are leaders in every community driving change. Many of them would never dream of calling themselves leaders, but they are.

99

Labour Party Conference,
24 September 2019

....

CHAPTER
FIVE

WORLD
AFFAIRS

If we do not take care of our planet and our environment, and of animals such as the whale, mankind will suffer and our planet will die because we have not cared for the natural environment that we all share.

Whaling debate, House of Commons, 2 March 1990

> **“**
> There is incontrovertible evidence that carbon dioxide emissions are increasing at an unprecedented rate. Unless we are able to reduce them, the consequences will be truly horrendous. **”**

House of Commons, 7 November 1990

66

The idea that nuclear weapons deter anyone is laughable and horrific.

Foreign affairs and defence debate,
House of Commons, 1 November 1991

99

66

We should be dedicating
ourselves to a peaceful world,
rather than arming ourselves for
war upon war upon war.

99

House of Commons, 18 October 1993

66

We want to live in a world that
is harmonious, but it will not be
harmonious if the gap between
the rich and poor widens.

99

International development debate,
House of Commons, 1 July 1997

66

I hope that we now recognize
that this planet cannot survive
unless we find an environmentally
sustainable form of development
and eradicate the gap between the
richest and poorest nations. **99**

International development debate,
House of Commons, 1 July 1997

> **“**
> This will set off a spiral of conflict, of hate, of misery, of desperation, that will fuel the wars, the conflict, the terrorism, the depression and the misery of future generations. **”**

Anti-war speech, Anti-Iraq War rally,
15 February 2003

> **“**
> 8,000 deaths in Afghanistan brought back none of those who died in the World Trade Center.
> **”**

Anti-war speech, Anti-Iraq War rally, 15 February 2003

66

There was no attempt whatsoever that I can see to arrest him [Osama bin Laden] and put him on trial, to go through that process. This was an assassination attempt, and is yet another tragedy, upon a tragedy, upon a tragedy. The World Trade Center was a tragedy, the attack on Afghanistan was a tragedy, the war in Iraq was a tragedy...

…Tens of thousands of people have died. Torture has come back on to the world stage, been canonized virtually into law by Guantánamo and Bagram. Can't we learn some lessons from this? Are we just going to sink deeper and deeper?

"

Iranian State television, May 2011

Russia has gone way beyond its legal powers to use bases in the Crimea. Sending unidentified forces into another country is clearly a violation of that country's sovereignty... Still, the hypocrisy of the West remains unbelievable...

…NATO has sought to expand since the end of the Cold War. It has increased its military capability and expenditure. It operates way beyond its original 1948 area and its attempt to encircle Russia is one of the big threats of our time. "

Morning Star, *4 March 2014*

66

We live in a time when there
are serious human rights abuses
all around the world... If we as
a country leave the European
Convention on Human Rights,
which is the human rights system
in Europe, what message will
that send to the rest of the world –
that we do not care about human
rights and that we do not think
they are important?

99

Britain in the world debate,
House of Commons, 1 June 2015

" We need a world of peace, not of war. We need a world of human rights and justice, not of injustice and imprisonment. We achieve those things not by greater militarization but by trying to promote peace, human rights and justice all over the world. **"**

Britain in the world debate, House of Commons, 1 June 2015

66

There is not going to be a peace process unless there are talks involving Israel, Hezbollah and Hamas, and I think everyone knows that.

99

Channel 4 News, 13 July 2015

66

Look, you don't make peace unless you talk to everybody. **99**

New Statesman, *29 July 2015*

66

I think NATO is a Cold War
product. I think NATO historically
should have shut up shop in 1990
along with the Warsaw Pact;
unfortunately, it didn't.

99

Financial Times, *23 August 2015*

66

I am opposed to the use of nuclear weapons. I am opposed to the holding of nuclear weapons. I want to see a nuclear-free world. I believe it is possible. I do not think we should be renewing Trident... I think we should be promoting an international nuclear weapons convention that would lead to a nuclear-free world.

99

BBC News, September 2015

Going to war creates a legacy
of bitterness and problems.
Let us be a force for change in
the world, a force for humanity
in the world, a force for peace in
the world, and a force that
recognizes we cannot go on like
this, with grotesque levels of global
inequality, grotesque threats...

...to our environment all around the world, without the rich and powerful governments stepping up to the plate to make sure our world becomes safer and better – and those people don't end up in poverty, in refugee camps, wasting their lives away. **"**

Labour leadership victory speech,
14 September 2015

66

Basically, on the question of
Europe, I want to see a
social Europe, a cohesive Europe,
a coherent Europe, not a free
market Europe.

99

BBC interview, 17 September 2015

66

There are five declared nuclear weapon states in the world. There are three others that have nuclear weapons. That is eight countries out of 192; 187 countries do not feel the need to have nuclear weapons to protect their security. Why should those five need them to protect their security? We are not in the Cold War any more.

99

Today *programme, Radio 4,*
30 September 2015

66 Look, if you believe in peace, you believe in human rights, you believe in justice and you believe in a foreign policy that sets those at the heart, rather than to militarily dominate the world... There are people who won't agree with that but will understand the need for peace and justice. **99**

On being asked, "What is security?" by Russian TV channel Russia Today, October 2015

I want a world of peace. I'm
not interested in bombs. I'm not
interested in wars. I'm interested
in peace.

Democracy Now!, *8 December 2015*

66

The idea that somehow or other you can deal with all the problems in the world by banning a particular religious group from entering the USA is offensive and absurd. **99**

Huffington Post UK, *19 December 2015*

66

[It is] perfectly possible to be
critical [of European Union
shortcomings] and still be
convinced we need to remain
a member.

99

Speech on the European Union,
14 April 2016

66

Our Jewish friends are no more responsible for the actions of Israel or the Netanyahu government than our Muslim friends are for those of various self-styled Islamic states or organizations.

99

Anti-Semitism speech, 30 June 2016

66

I will continue – as Labour leader –
to pursue the causes of peace
and justice in Israel-Palestine, the
wider Middle East and all over the
world. But those who claim to do
so with hateful or inflammatory
language do no service to anyone,
especially dispossessed and
oppressed people in need of
better advocacy.

99

Anti-Semitism speech, 30 June 2016

> **"**
> I would not take a decision that kills millions of people, I do not believe the threat of mass murder is a legitimate way to go about dealing with international relations.
> **"**

Opposing Trident renewal, House of Commons debate, 18 July 2016

> **"**
> It is time we recognized the huge contribution that migration has made to the economic growth of this country. **"**

Twitter, 2 September 2016

❝

The government appears to be waiting for instructions from President Donald Trump on how to proceed. Britain should press for an independent UN-led investigation of last weekend's horrific chemical weapons attack so that those responsible can be held to account.

❞

On the use of chemical weapons in Syria, 13 April 2018

66

Our environment is under threat...
there is no hiding place, ultimately,
from foul air, from dirty seas, from
polluted rivers. There's no hiding
place from the destruction of our
natural world for any of us – unless
we work together to protect it
and our environment and our
sustainability.

99

Speech to anti-Trump protesters,
London, 13 July 2018

66

When a government condemns children because they're Mexican or Guatemalan or from somewhere else in Central America, that is a breach of every international convention that I understand.

99

Speech to anti-Trump protesters, London, 13 July 2018

When a major country says it wants to walk away from the UN Council on Human Rights, I say, 'Sorry, you are wrong. Human rights belong to all of us.'

Speech to anti-Trump protesters, London, 13 July 2018

66

Never forget that protest and activism eventually leads to change. I want to live in a world that thrives, that survives.

99

Speech to anti-Trump protesters, London, 4 June 2019

> **66**
> There is nothing wrong with
> my heart except for wanting a
> peaceful world.
> **99**

The Andrew Marr Show,
29 September 2019

CHAPTER
SIX

OBSERVATIONS

" I started wearing a beard when I was 19 and living in Jamaica; they called me Mr Beardman. **"**

On winning the Beard Liberation Front's Beard of the Year award in 2002

66

Riding a bicycle is the summit of
human endeavour – an almost
neutral environmental effect
coupled with the ability to travel
substantial distances without
disturbing anybody. The bike is the
perfect marriage of technology
and human energy.

99

The Guardian, *14 February 2007*

66

I still have the Triumph Palm Beach
I was given for Christmas when I
was 11. By today's standards, it
is heavy and slow, but it was my
pride and joy at the time.

99

The Guardian, *14 February 2007*

I do not own a car, and my main form of travel to Westminster and in my constituency is by bicycle. I also take my bike on trains to meetings in other parts of the country, which enables me to see other cities and the other parts of the country.

The Guardian, *14 February 2007*

66

I don't spend a lot of money,
I lead a very normal life.

The Guardian, *17 June 2015*

> **❝**
> Mum and Dad met campaigning
> on the Spanish civil war. Both were
> active peace campaigners. **❞**

The Guardian, *17 June 2015*

66

Are super-rich people actually happy with being super-rich? I would want the super-rich to pay properly their share of the needs of the rest of the community.

99

Speaking to Channel 4, 13 July 2015

66

I've got lots of stamina; don't worry about that. I cycle every day – it's OK.

New Statesman, *29 July 2015*

66

There have been some amazing statements that have come out about me in the past few days. Apparently people know what's going on in my mind so I don't need to think any more. I just read the papers.

99

New Statesman, *29 July 2015*

“

It's deeply embarrassing. I think it's a bit of a joke actually.

On being asked about his new sex symbol status, Evening Standard, *5 August 2015*

”

> **"** Diversity in media is something that is intrinsic to a democratic society. We do not want the whole media owned by one person. **"**

Financial Times, *August 2015*

66

I am vegetarian. ... I became one at 20 when I was working on a pig farm. I got attached to the pigs and I couldn't stand the thought that they would have to go off to be slaughtered.

99

Camden New Journal, *13 August 2015*

66

Sure, I've met with people I don't agree with.

99

On being asked about his pro-Palestinian campaigning, Financial Times, *23 August 2015*

---

66 I think we can spend too much time worrying about polls. **99**

The Guardian, *26 September 2015*

> **"** I have always worked long hours and very hard. It is the way I am. Same as always. Up about seven and get to bed about 12 to 1, something like that. **"**

The Guardian, *26 September 2015*

66

I have always had a very busy life.
The difference is that a lot more
people are helping advise me what
to do, and a lot more people are
observing what I do. But in terms
of time and working schedule, it is
not that different from my normal
working week.

99

The Guardian, *26 September 2015*

66

My view is the questions in Parliament should be the questions that people out there want asked.

99

Newsbeat, *BBC One, 29 September 2015*

66

I've been in Parliament since 1983, and I've been involved in many issues over the time.

99

Democracy Now!, *8 December 2015*

66

Tony Benn and I were very close, very close friends for 30, 40 years. We talked to each other a great deal, and we were great friends. And I was with him shortly before he died, talking about prospects of the world and prospects for peace. And I'm very sad that he's gone.

99

Democracy Now!, *8 December 2015*

" Parliament is supposed to be serious. It's not a place for jingoistic cheering. **"**

In response to Hilary Benn's House of Commons speech on Syria, 20 December 2015

66

I respect all faiths, I probably spend more time going to religious services than most people, of all types. I go to synagogues, I go to mosques, I go to temples, I go to churches, and I have many humanistic friends and I have many atheist friends. I respect them all.

99

Huffington Post, *20 December 2015*

Because I've never had any higher
education of any sort, I've never
held in awe those who have had it
or have a sense of superiority over
those who don't.

Red Pepper, 21 December 2015

66

I think back to the Tony Benn deputy leadership campaign in 1981. I think of the miners' strike in 1984. I think back to the industrial democracy movement in the early 1970s. All of which I was very involved with, but they would have been so much more successful and so much better if we'd had better forms of communication.

99

Red Pepper, 21 December 2015

66

I have this 18th-century religious view that there is some good in everybody. Sometimes you have to search quite hard for it. Sometimes it's very hard to find and you wonder if it really is there.

99

Red Pepper, 21 December 2015

"
Life is life. Some of the wisest
people you meet are sweeping
our streets.
"

Red Pepper, 21 December 2015

66

I do think the public want to
see politicians acting in a different
way. What's brought young people
into our campaign is that they were
written off by political parties but
they had never written off politics,
and what we have is a huge
number of young people, very
enthusiastic and brimming with
ideas. Those ideas have got to
be heard.

99

Newsbeat, *29 December 2015*

66

Of course I want to be
[prime minister].

Channel 4 News, *24 June 2016*

66

I'm totally anti-sugar on
health grounds, so eat very few
biscuits, but if forced to accept
one, it's always a pleasure to
have a shortbread.

99

*On being asked what his favourite
biscuit was, Mumsnet Q&A, 2016*

66

The man's not hot.

99

On being asked if he wanted to take his jacket off and referencing Roadman Shaq's "Man's Not Hot", Labour Party Conference, 28 September 2017

66

I would love to say England, but I doubt it. Brazil or Germany.

On being asked who he thought would win the 2018 FIFA World Cup

99

> **We live in a very unequal society.**

The Guardian, *17 June 2015*